OAuth

Getting Started in Web-API Security

by Matthias Biehl

API University Series
www.api-university.com

API-University Press

Copyright © 2014, 2015, 2016 by Matthias Biehl
All rights reserved, including the right to reproduce
this book or portions thereof in any form whatsoever.

ISBN-13: 978-1507800911
ISBN-10: 1507800916

Table of Contents

SUMMARY	7
WHO SHOULD READ THIS BOOK?	8
1 INTRODUCTION	**10**
1.1 THE PASSWORD ANTI-PATTERN	11
1.2 WHAT IS OAUTH 2?	12
1.3 TERMS	13
2 OAUTH ACTORS	**15**
2.1 OAUTH PROVIDER	16
2.2 RESOURCE PROVIDER	17
2.3 RESOURCE OWNER	18
2.4 CLIENT	19
2.5 ACTORS IN A COMPLETE OAUTH SOLUTION	19
3 OAUTH ENDPOINTS	**22**
3.1 AUTHORIZATION ENDPOINT	22
3.2 TOKEN ENDPOINT	22
3.3 REDIRECT ENDPOINT	23
4 OAUTH TOKENS	**26**
4.1 ACCESS TOKEN	26
4.2 REFRESH TOKEN	27
4.3 AUTHORIZATION CODE	27
4.4 TOKEN ATTRIBUTES	28
4.4.1 SCOPES	28
4.4.2 USER DEFINED ATTRIBUTES	29

5 OAUTH FLOWS	**30**
5.1 AUTHORIZATION CODE FLOW	**32**
5.1.1 USAGE SCENARIO	32
5.1.2 FEATURES	33
5.1.3 PREPARATION	34
5.1.4 AUTHORIZATION CODE FLOWS	34
5.1.5 FIRST TIME AUTHORIZATION CODE FLOW	35
5.1.6 FOLLOW-UP AUTHORIZATION CODE FLOW	44
5.2 IMPLICIT FLOW	**47**
5.2.1 USAGE SCENARIO	47
5.2.2 FEATURES	47
5.2.3 PREPARATION	48
5.2.4 SEQUENCE DIAGRAMS	48
5.3 RESOURCE OWNER PASSWORD CREDENTIALS FLOW	**52**
5.3.1 USAGE SCENARIO	52
5.3.2 FEATURES	53
5.3.3 PREPARATION	54
5.3.4 SEQUENCE DIAGRAMS	55
5.4 CLIENT CREDENTIALS FLOW	**59**
5.4.1 USAGE SCENARIO	59
5.4.2 FEATURES	59
5.4.3 PREPARATION	60
5.4.4 SEQUENCE DIAGRAMS	60
6 EXTENSIONS OF OAUTH	**64**
6.1 OPENID CONNECT PROFILE	**64**
6.1.1 USAGE SCENARIO	64
6.1.2 SEQUENCE DIAGRAMS	65
6.2 SAML 2 BEARER ASSERTION PROFILE	**71**
6.2.1 USAGE SCENARIO	71
6.2.2 SEQUENCE DIAGRAM	71
7 CONSIDERATIONS FOR SECURE OAUTH 2	**76**
7.1 LEVEL OF SECURITY PROVIDED BY OAUTH 2	**76**

7.1.1 Security of Different OAuth Flows	76
7.1.2 Client Authentication	77
7.1.3 User Authentication	77
7.1.4 Token-based Authorization	77
7.2 Securing Access Tokens and Client Credentials	**78**
7.2.1 Secure Transmission of Tokens and Client Credentials	78
7.2.2 Secure Storage of Tokens and Client Credentials	78
7.2.3 Resource Owner Access to Tokens	79
7.3 Revocation of Access Tokens	**80**
8 BACKMATTER	**82**
Feedback	82
About the Author	82
Other Products by the Author	83
API Architecture and Design Book	83
OAuth 2.0 Online Course	85
References	85
Image Sources	86

Summary

This book offers an introduction to API Security with OAuth 2.0. In less than 80 pages you will gain an overview of the capabilities of OAuth. You will learn the core concepts of OAuth. You will get to know all 4 OAuth Flows that are used in cloud solutions and mobile apps.

If you have tried to read the official OAuth specification, you may get the impression that OAuth is complicated. This book explains OAuth in simple terms. The different OAuth Flows are visualized graphically using sequence diagrams. The diagrams allow you to see the big picture of the various OAuth interactions. This high-level overview is complemented with a rich set of example requests and responses and an explanation of the technical details.

In the book the challenges and benefits of OAuth are presented, followed by an explanation of the technical concepts of OAuth. The technical concepts include the actors, endpoints, tokens and the four OAuth flows. Each flow is described in detail, including the use cases for each flow.

Extensions of OAuth - so called profiles - are presented, such as OpenID Connect and the SAML2 Bearer Profile. Sequence diagrams are presented to explain the necessary interactions.

Who should read this book?

You do not have the time to read long books? This book provides an overview, the core concepts, without getting lost in the small-small details. This book provides all the necessary information to get started with OAuth in less than 80 pages.

You believe OAuth is complicated? OAuth may seem complicated with flows and redirects going back and forth. This book will give you clarity by introducing the seemingly complicated material by many illustrations. These illustrations clearly show all the involved interaction parties and the messages they exchange.

You want to learn the OAuth concepts efficiently? This book uses many illustrations and sequence diagrams. A good diagram says more than 1000 words.

You want to learn the difference between OAuth and OpenID Connect? You wonder when the two concepts are used, what they have in common and what is different between them. This book will help you answer this question.

You want to use OAuth in your mobile app? If you want to access resources that are protected by OAuth, you need to get a token first, before you can access the resource. For this, you need to understand the OAuth flows and the dependencies between the steps of the flows.

You want to use OAuth to protect your APIs? OAuth is perfectly suited to protect your APIs. You can learn which OAuth endpoints need to be provided and which checks need to be made within the protected APIs.

1 Introduction

People have gotten a bit sensitive about internet security and privacy. "Mobile apps, web-APIs and Cloud Services - yes, I like and use them, but ... is my data really secure there? Can I control what happens to my data and who can access is?" These and many related questions are top-of-mind for many cloud and mobile users. And, who can blame them? With the recent incidents of compromised accounts and stolen passwords, these types of question are more than justified. Organizations that offer mobile apps and cloud services have to address these questions of their users. These organizations are not any longer only web-startups, Google and Facebook. Today, the business of almost every industry is transforming into a digital business. Businesses across the different industries thus need to think about information security. To differentiate, more and more traditional businesses increasingly create digital services for their customers.

That is why all types of businesses need to face the security questions of their users. Users demand the responsible processing, storing and transmission of their data – and companies have to react now. To win the trust of their customers and users, organizations need to take the concerns of their users seriously. They can do this by building on established standards instead of building proprietary solutions.

In the context of web-APIs, mobile apps and cloud services, there are two established standards for authentication and authorization: OAuth 2 and OpenID Connect. But which standard should be used in a given scenario? How does the technology work? Which experiences have been gathered from practical use of these technologies?

1.1 The Password Anti-Pattern

Let us start with an example: Sarah uses the mobile app of her car insurance to register a claim for a minor accident. On the mobile app of her insurance company, she first has to authenticate by entering her username and password. Because entering passwords is cumbersome, the mobile app saves the credentials on the mobile.

A second example: Tim wants his tweets from Twitter to appear on LinkedIn automatically to stay in touch with his business contacts. To realize this functionality, LinkedIn would need to have access to Tim's Twitter account. The simplistic solution would be to provide LinkedIn with the credentials of Twitter, so LinkedIn can directly access Tim's tweets.

However, both "solutions" would be quite a security risk, since Sarah's password is saved unprotected on the mobile and Tim's password is provided to another cloud service. Both instances are examples of the "Password Anti-Pattern". In practice, this solution cannot be used.

1.2 What is OAuth 2?

OAuth 2 is a standard for delegating authorization for accessing resources via HTTP.

OAuth 2 offers a solution for the scenarios of the examples above without the risks of the password anti-pattern. With OAuth 2 we can give access rights to the mobile app, without providing the password. Instead, a token is handed to the app. The token represents the access rights for a subset of the data, for a short time frame. To obtain the token, the user first logs in on the website of the OAuth server. The generated token can be an authorization code, an access token or a refresh token. An access token allows access to a resource during a limited time period. In case the token gets compromised, the access rights associated with the token can be revoked.

Sarah and Tim from the previous example will not notice any difference. The user experience is roughly the same, whether OAuth is used or not. The important difference: Sarah and Tim can use their mobile apps and cloud apps in a secure manner, if OAuth is used under the hood.

In fact, OAuth is under the hood of many modern cloud, mobile and web applications. The end user can notice a few advantages. The advantages are that they have a fine-granular control over the access to their data, do not need to give their password to third parties, and if they should lose their mobile, they can remotely revoke all OAuth tokens which are stored on the lost device.

OAuth 2 is a standard that is used in mobile integration use cases, when mobile apps need to communicate securely with server-side backend systems. OAuth 2 is also a standard for securing APIs. It is for example used in the APIs offered by Google, Twitter, LinkedIn, Amazon and Ebay. Most cloud-based Software-as-a-Service offerings use OAuth for protecting their services and the data of their users.

OAuth 2 is specified and standardized by the IETF in RFC6749 (http://tools.ietf.org/html/rfc6749). OAuth 1 has been replaced by OAuth 2, is outdated and not presented here. This is why we use the short form OAuth to refer to OAuth 2.

1.3 Terms

Two similar terms -- authentication and authorization -- are used in the context of OAuth and API Security. To understand the details of OAuth, it is essential to know the distinction between the two:

Authentication is a concept for answering the question: Who are you? Authentication provides a method for providing proof for the claimed identity.

Authorization is a concept that answers the question: What are you allowed to do? Authorization provides the rights assigned to the confirmed identity, for example access rights. For OAuth, authentication is a precondition for proper authorization.

13

OAuth relies on authentication and authorization but does neither. This can be confusing, since the name "OAuth" suggests that it might be related to one of them.

OAuth 2 is a framework for delegation of HTTP-based access. Authentication is performed by another component, for example by the mechanisms of a login page. Authorization needs to be performed by the API, which uses the token and information related to the token for authorizing access to the protected resource.

2 OAuth Actors

OAuth is designed for distributed systems that consist of several actors with distinct roles. Just like the actors in a movie play specific roles so the story can evolve, each actor in an OAuth flow takes on a specific role in the overall OAuth solution. The following actors can be found in all OAuth-based interactions:

- OAuth Provider (also known as OAuth server or authorization server)
- Resource Provider (usually a set of web APIs)
- Resource Owner (also known as user)
- Client (usually a cloud app or mobile app)

In this chapter we characterize each of the four OAuth actors. Understanding each OAuth actor will help you to map the OAuth concepts to the components in your specific software project.

2.1 OAuth Provider

The OAuth provider (also known as OAuth server or authorization server) consists of:

- An authentication component (such as a login page and an identity provider)
- A component (consent server) for requesting the authenticated user's consent for the delegation of access rights to the client
- A token-management infrastructure (such as a database).

Let me give you an example: Tim wants that his tweets from Twitter appear automatically on LinkedIn so he can stay in touch with his business contacts. In this example the OAuth provider would be a component which is made available by Twitter as the service provider.

In this book the OAuth provider is visualized as follows:

2.2 Resource Provider

The resource provider makes a protected resource available. The resource may be data or a service and is often offered in the form of a web API, which in turn offers the protected data. The web-API has to ensure that only authenticated and authorized users can in fact access the data. It does this by requiring an OAuth access token as part of the request. For each incoming request the web-API first needs to check the validity of the provided access token. Only requests with valid access tokens will be allowed to access the resource.

In the example introduced earlier, LinkedIn attempts to access a Twitter tweet. Thus Twitter is the resource provider in this scenario.

In this book the resource provider is visualized as follows:

17

2.3 Resource Owner

The resource owner is the owner of the protected resource. For example the user of Twitter is the owner of his profile data and the tweets written by him. The resource owner can access the data he owns directly on Twitter. However, in the context of OAuth it is not the direct access by the resource owner, which is relevant. Relevant in the context of OAuth, is the indirect access to the data by a third party (the client).

The resource owner delegates his access rights to the third party (the client). Through this delegation the resource owner allows the third party (the client) to access his data. The third party accesses the data in the name of the resource owner.

In the example introduced earlier, Tim wants that his LinkedIn account can access his tweets on Twitter. Thus Tim is the resource owner in this scenario.

In this book the resource owner is depicted as follows:

2.4 Client

The client is an application that attempts to access a protected resource. The client can be a web application, a mobile app or a cloud app.

In the example introduced earlier, LinkedIn attempts to access Twitter tweets. Thus LinkedIn is the client in this scenario.

Since the client is usually a mobile app or a cloud app, it is visualized as follows:

2.5 Actors in a Complete OAuth Solution

In a complete OAuth solution all types of actors can be found. In some scenarios, however, a software component can have the roles of several actors.

In the example introduced earlier, Tim's LinkedIn account attempts to access Tim's Twitter tweets. In this scenario LinkedIn is the client, Tim is the resource owner, Twitter is the resource provider and Twitter is also the OAuth provider.

3 OAuth Endpoints

An OAuth endpoint is a service with a defined behavior and address. In a typical OAuth scenario, three endpoints are used, that interact in a defined manner. The endpoints are realized as RESTful services.

3.1 Authorization Endpoint

The authorization endpoint is a service offered by the OAuth provider. In more exact terms, it is a part of the consent server inside the OAuth provider. It authenticates the resource owner using any typical authentication method, such as username and password. After authentication, the resource owner is explicitly asked to confirm the delegation of his access rights for the protected resources. The authorization endpoint sends a confirmation of the authentication and of the access delegation to the redirect endpoint. This confirmation is called an authorization code. The authorization endpoint is usually invoked by the client before attempting to access a new resource.

3.2 Token Endpoint

The token endpoint is a service offered by the OAuth provider. It produces OAuth tokens, namely access tokens and refresh tokens and returns them in the form of a JSON object to the requester.

Of course, not everyone can request the tokens on the token endpoint. Access to the token endpoint is protected by HTTP basic authorization. The idea is that the token endpoint can only be called by clients that are known to the OAuth provider. The username used by the client is called ClientID and the password is called ClientSecret.

Clients have to register with the OAuth provider in order to receive a ClientID and a ClientSecret. The client registration, however, is not part of the token endpoint.

3.3 Redirect Endpoint

The redirect endpoint is a service offered by the client. The response produced by the authorization endpoint is sent to the redirect endpoint. The redirect endpoint is not called directly, but indirectly by a HTTP-redirect command (HTTP status code 302). The answer of the authorization endpoint contains an HTTP-redirect to the address of the redirect endpoint. The address of the redirect endpoint is transferred in the location header.

The authorization code produced by the authorization endpoint is attached to the URI of the redirect endpoint in the form of a query parameter. An example: If the URI of the redirect endpoint is http://www.mydomain.de/service the authorization endpoint sends a status code 302 along with the HTTP location header http://www.mydomain.de/service?code=wHFZhj712 back to the requestor. If the HTTP-redirect is executed, e.g. when it is sent to a browser, the redirect endpoint is called. The redirect endpoint receives all query parameters and thus can evaluate the authorization code. Using this mechanism the client can get hold of the authorization code. The client needs the authorization code to request an access token from the token endpoint.

4 OAuth Tokens

OAuth tokens are identifiers used in OAuth flows. The holder of the token has the access rights associated with the token. It is thus important to keep the access tokens confidential. One way to keep access tokens confidential is the exclusive use of transport layer security for all communication involving tokens.

The information about the tokens is stored in a database of the OAuth provider. They are unique, long strings of random characters. The tokens do not contain any encoded user data.

One can distinguish several types of OAuth tokens and codes.

4.1 Access Token

Access tokens are used by the client to access resources. The client sends the access token to the resource server when accessing the protected resource. The validity of the access token is limited to a short period (e.g. 24 hours). During the period of validity the same access token can be reused in any number of requests.

OAuth access tokens are bearer tokens. The holder of the token has the access rights associated with the tokens. The identity of the holder of the token is not checked any further.

As long as no OAuth federation is available, access tokens can only be verified by the OAuth provider that generated them.

4.2 Refresh Token

The refresh token has a period of validity that is longer than that of the access token (e.g. 30 days). It can be used to request a new access token after the access token has expired. When requesting an access token with a refresh token, the credentials do not have to be entered, so that it can be implemented as a process that is transparent for the resource owner. Refresh tokens are sent by the client to the token endpoint of the OAuth server. Refresh tokens are never sent to the resource server directly. Access to the resources is only possible with an access token.

4.3 Authorization Code

The OAuth provider creates an authorization code and sends it to the client after successfully authenticating the resource owner and getting the consent of the resource owner for delegating the access. The authorization code is thus a confirmation of the successful authentication and of the resource owner's consent.

The validity of the authorization code is usually limited to a couple of minutes. This is just enough time, so the client can use the authorization code to request an access token from the token endpoint.

The authorization code can only be processed by the token endpoint of the OAuth server. It will never be sent directly to the resource provider.

4.4 Token Attributes

4.4.1 Scopes

OAuth tokens are used as a confirmation for the delegation of access rights. Through delegation, the holder of the token, usually the client, has received a set of access rights, which are associated with the token. The token usually represents a set of access rights. But what if more fine-grained control over the data is required?

Fine-grained access can be realized by scopes. Each scope represents a specific access right. Scopes are realized as an attribute of the OAuth token. They are typically set by the authorization endpoint when the token is requested. Consecutive tokens that have been created using refresh tokens inherit all the scopes.

Scopes need to be managed properly to avoid confusion. The name of the scope can be used to indicate the business object that the scope grants access too. In addition, the name of the scope can indicate what type of access is provided, such as reading or writing (e.g. read-email and write-email). If no such indication is provided, it can be assumed that the scope grants both reading and writing access.

Scopes are typically bundled. When requesting a new OAuth token, the client can request a set of scopes. For different clients, a different set of scopes can be bundled.

4.4.2 User Defined Attributes

Some OAuth servers provide the possibility to create attributes and associate them with OAuth tokens. Sometimes people talk about "storing attributes on the token", however, this rather means associating attributes with the token. In contrast to the OAuth tokens, the JSON web tokens actually contain encrypted and encoded user data.

That way, the OAuth token can potentially be used as a session object for preserving state in between calls. While this feature is practical, this is not compatible with the principles of RESTful design. The recommendation is thus to limit the use of user-defined attributes on OAuth tokens and only use them if really necessary.

5 OAuth Flows

So far, we have introduced the components of an OAuth solution, comprising the actors, endpoints and tokens. These components can only be used in a sensible manner when they interact with each other.

In a movie, the interaction between the actors follows a story line, which is described in the movie script. In a similar manner, the interaction between the OAuth actors and components is described by so called OAuth flows.

OAuth flows describe the sequences of requests and responses exchanged among the OAuth actors and endpoints. During these interactions, credentials and tokens are requested, created, delivered, verified, updated and revoked. The underlying philosophy of the OAuth flows is to provide a high degree of security by checking the identity of each OAuth actor involved in the flow.

Depending on the different requirements of a given usage scenario, actors and endpoints can interact according to the rules set by the different flows. One typically distinguishes the following four OAuth flows, which are defined in the standard:

- The Authorization Code Flow, also known as 3-legged OAuth, is the default OAuth flow. It is also the most secure OAuth flow. A prerequisite for using this flow is, that the client has a possibility for secure storage of ClientID and ClientSecret. All other OAuth flows are simplifications of this default flow.

- The Implicit Flow is used, when the client cannot securely store ClientID, ClientSecret or OAuth tokens. This is for example the case when the client is written in client-side JavaScript. The limitation of this flow is the shorter validity of the generated tokens.

- The Resource Owner Password Credentials Flow is used when the resource owner can entrust the password to the client.

- The Client Credentials Flow, also known as 2-legged OAuth, is applied when the client is also the resource owner.

In the following we describe all four OAuth flows. Since the authorization code flow is the default flow and the most complete flow, it is described first with the most detailed description. The remaining flows have many commonalities with the authorization code flow. To avoid repetition, the similarities are not repeated, but the differences are pointed out.

5.1 Authorization Code Flow

The authorization code flow is also called 3-legged OAuth. The reason for this naming is that this flow enables checking the identity of the three involved actors: OAuth server, resource owner and client.

The OAuth server authenticates the resource owner by the username and password that are provided interactively by the resource owner.

The OAuth server authenticates the client by his ClientID and ClientSecret, which are transmitted in the HTTP header. The HTTP basic authorization mechanism is used, which reads the credential from the HTTP field "authorization".

The client authenticates the OAuth server by checking its certificate and URL.

5.1.1 Usage Scenario

When using this flow, secure storage for tokens, ClientID and ClientSecret needs to be provided by the client. Secure storage can for example be provided, if the client is implemented as a server-side web application. Tokens can be stored for example in a protected database, which is not accessible for any outside attackers.

Secure storage is not necessarily provided by applications written in client-side JavaScript, such as simple HTML5-based mobile apps. Using the authorization code flow for these types of clients is not recommended. More information about security consideration for OAuth is provided in chapter 7.

5.1.2 Features

The main feature of this OAuth flow is its relatively high level of security:

- The access token is not flowing through the browser
- The username and password of the resource owners are not known to the client.
- Moreover it is secure, since the identities of all 3 communication partners are assured:
- The identity of the OAuth server is assured by the URL and the SSL certificate of the OAuth server.
- The identity of the resource owner is assured by the authentication of the resource owner. The resource owner has to prove his identity with login and password towards the OAuth consent server.
- The identity of the client is assured, since the client authenticates at the OAuth consent server. Only the client knows ClientID and ClientSecret.
- Another feature of this flow is the convenience it provides for the resource owner: The use of refresh tokens allows granting access for a longer period of time, without requiring the resource owner to re-authenticate.

5.1.3 Preparation

Before the regular OAuth flow can be started, the client has to register with the OAuth server. After successful registration the client receives a ClientID and a ClientSecret. ClientID and ClientSecret are used when creating new tokens, to confirm the identity of the client. The manner in which registration for ClientID and ClientSecret takes place is not regulated by the standard. In practice, the registration takes place on a website or a self-service portal of the OAuth server.

5.1.4 Authorization Code Flows

The OAuth flows are described by a series of sequence diagrams. Each sequence diagram covers one use case for a specific endpoint.

The following actors take part in the authorization code flow:

- The resource owner (on the left) wants to use a mobile or web app.
- The mobile or web app (on the middle-left) takes on the role of the client and accesses the protected services or APIs (on the right).
- The protected services or APIs (on the right) act as resource providers.
- The OAuth provider (on the middle-right) creates the tokens and codes before it sends them back to the client.

There are actually two types of authorization code flows. One flow for first-time access, in case the client does not have any tokens from previous interactions. The resource owner will have to log in by providing his credentials.

Alternatively, there is a follow-up access, which is used if the client has previously gained access. If the access token of the previous interaction has expired, but the refresh token is still valid, the client can use the refresh token to obtain a new access token. The advantage of the follow-up flow is that it is more convenient for the resource owner, since she is not required to enter her credentials. The follow-up flow is in fact transparent to the resource owner and only involves the client and the OAuth provider.

5.1.5 First Time Authorization Code Flow

The first-time flow contains the following steps:

- Get the authorization code: The client requests an authorization code from the authorization endpoint of the OAuth provider.
- Get the token: The client requests a token from the token endpoint of the OAuth provider using the authorization code.
- Access the protected resource: The client accesses the resource from the resource provider using the access token.

5.1.5.1 Authorization Endpoint

The authorization endpoint is used to provide the client with an authorization code. This is a preparation for later being able to request access and refresh tokens.

The authorization code is a confirmation of the successful authentication of the resource owner and is valid for a short period of time only. The client cannot access the resource with the authorization code alone. The authorization code can only be used to request an access and refresh token from the token endpoint.

The client sends his request to the authorization endpoint of the OAuth server using an HTTP GET. The consent server, which is a part of the OAuth server, provides the resource owner with an authentication dialog allowing the resource owner to authenticate. This login page is usually realized as a web page. If login or single-sign-on (SSO) web pages already exist in the organization, these existing authentication dialogs and authentication methods can be reused by the consent server.

The authentication is typically based on a username and password, but is not limited to it. The OAuth standard does not prescribe any particular authentication mechanism. Recommended is a two-factor authentication mechanism, using a password as the first factor and a text message sent to the mobile of the user as the second factor. A successful authentication confirms that the user is actually the resource owner.

After authentication, the consent server informs the resource owner in detail about the access rights that will be delegated to the client. Ideally the access rights are structured in a fine-granular way and can thus be granted or revoked in a fine-granular way. The consent server offers the possibility for reviewing the list of delegated access rights to the resource owner. On this web page, the resource owner has the possibility to accept or deny the delegation of his access rights.

How does the consent server know, which access rights should be delegated to the client? The consent server presents the list of access rights, which were requested by the client when calling the authorization endpoint. In the request, an access right is usually represented by the concept of an OAuth scope. The scope parameter, which the client provides to the OAuth server, contains a list of space-separated scopes. The client requests access rights by adding a list of scopes to the request to the authorization endpoint.

The client is involved in neither the authentication nor the consent interaction. Only the authorization endpoint and the resource owner are involved in these interactions. An advantage of this flow is that the credentials of the resource owner are kept secret from the client.

If the client sends several requests to the authorization endpoint, it might be difficult to map the resulting authorization code to the request that created it. This issue is solved by the state parameter. It is used to correlate the request with the corresponding response. The OAuth server just pipes the state parameter received as input to the output without processing it.

The output created by the authorization endpoint is unusual for a service. It is unusual, since it does not return a payload and a 200 OK status code. Instead, the authorization endpoint returns a 302 Moved Permanently status code with an HTTP location header. The location header contains a URL. The real response, which is the authorization code, is a query parameter in this URL. In the same manner, the state parameter, which is used by the client to correlate request and response, is contained as a query parameter in the URL. The base path of the URL, the so-called redirect URL, was registered with the OAuth server during the initial client registration. The registered URL is compared to the redirect_uri, which was supplied as an input parameter. Only if both URLs are equal, the authorization endpoint will deliver the authorization code to the client.

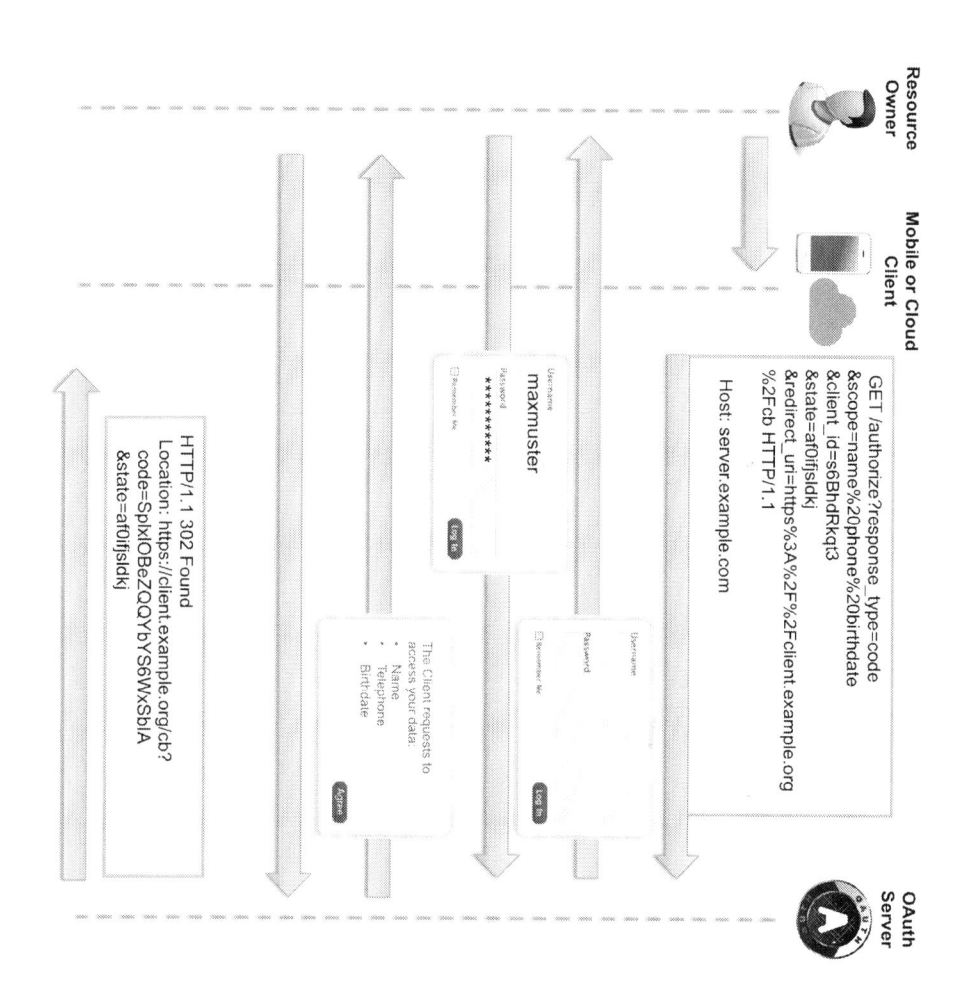

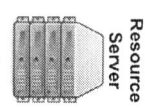

To identify the client, the ClientID needs to be provided as part of the request. It may be provided as an HTTP header parameter or as a query parameter At this point, the ClientSecret is not required. The authorization endpoint is publicly accessible and not protected.

Keep in mind that the authorization code is only valid for a short period of time and cannot be used directly for gaining access to the protected resource. To gain access to the protected resource, an access token has to be requested from the token endpoint using the authorization code.

5.1.5.2 Token Endpoint

The token endpoint is a part of the OAuth server and provides a token-object containing an access token and a refresh token. The client can request them using the authorization code, which was received from the authorization endpoint.

The token endpoint is protected by HTTP basic authorization. For this endpoint it is not the resource owner who has to authenticate, but the client. The client authenticates using HTTP basic authorization with the ClientID as username and the ClientSecret as password. Both were provided during the client registration process. The HTTP header field "Authorization" is used with the value "Basic ClientID:ClientSecret", where ClientID:ClientSecret need to be base64 encoded.

In summary, the client needs to authenticate and send the authorization code as a query parameter. The response is a JSON object containing the access token, refresh token and the remaining validity period.

	Resource Owner	Mobile or Cloud Client	OAuth Server	Resource Server

```
POST /token HTTP/1.1
Host: server.example.com
Content-Type: application/x-www-form-urlencoded
Authorization: Basic czZCaGRSa3F0MzpnWDFm

grant_type=authorization_code
&code=SplxlOBeZQQYbYS6WxSblA
```

```
HTTP/1.1 200 OK
Content-Type: application/json
{
  "access_token": "SlAV32hkKG",
  "token_type": "Bearer",
  "refresh_token": "8xLOxBtZp8",
  "expires_in": 3600
}
```

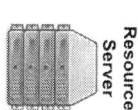

41

5.1.5.3 Resource Access

The resource provider protects the access to the resources. Any access to this resource needs to be authorized using an access token. The resource provider verifies the access token before granting access. If the access token is valid, the requested resource is returned. If the access token is invalid, an error code is returned.

The token verification service, which is used by the resource provider, is a built-in service of the OAuth provider. If the access token is invalid, in general the status code 401 (Unauthorized) is returned. However, if the access token is expired, the status code 403 (Forbidden) is returned. This indicates to the client, that first a new access token has to be requested, either by going back to the authorization endpoint, or preferably, if a valid refresh token is available by using the token endpoint directly. The advantage of the second option is that the resource owner does not need to authenticate again.

In the picture the protected resource is an API. The access token is transmitted as a bearer token in the authorization HTTP header field. The exact syntax is shown in the picture.

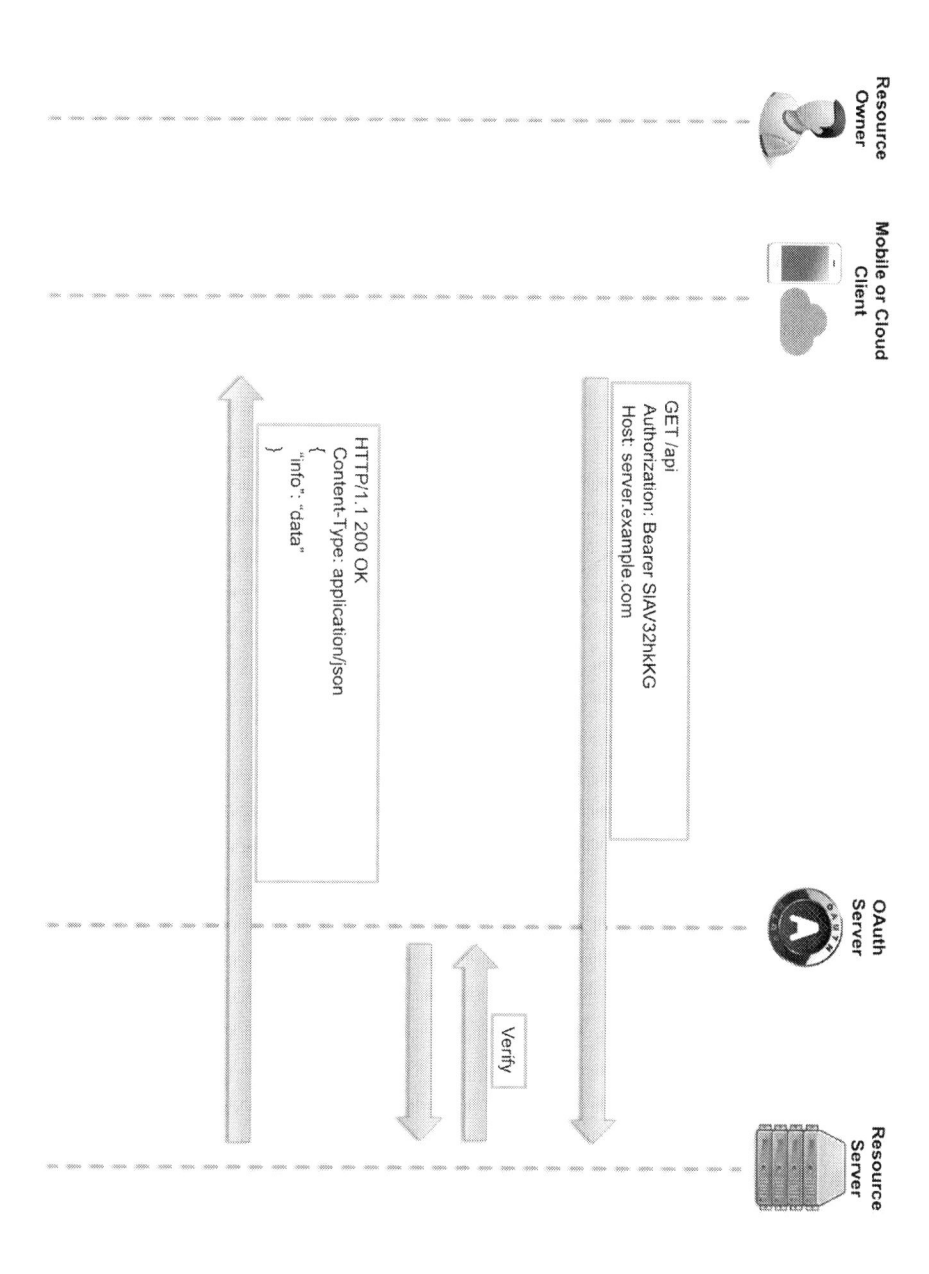

5.1.6 Follow-up Authorization Code Flow

The follow-up flow is used when the access token has expired and a valid refresh token is available. The refresh token is used to request a new access token and refresh token. The flow contains the following steps:

- Get a new token: the client requests a token from the token endpoint of the OAuth provider using the refresh token
- Access the protected resource: the client accesses the resource from the resource provider using the access token

5.1.6.1 Token Endpoint (Refresh)

In case the access token has expired and the client has a valid refresh token, a new access token can be requested from the token endpoint using HTTP POST. The client simply provides the refresh token instead of the authorization code. The advantage of this flow is that it is convenient for the resource owner. Using this flow, the resource owner does not need to authenticate again.

In the picture a sample request to the token endpoint is depicted:

- The client needs to authenticate using the base64 encoded ClientID:ClientSecret in the Authorization HTTP header field.
- The two query parameters to the token endpoint are the parameter grant_type, which is set to the value refresh_token and the parameter refresh_token, which

contains the actual refresh token.
- The successful response contains a JSON object with a new access token, a new refresh token and the new validity period of the access token.

```
Resource Server

OAuth Server

Mobile or Cloud Client

Resource Owner
```

POST /token HTTP/1.1
Host: server.example.com
Content-Type: application/x-www-form-urlencoded
Authorization: Basic czZCaGRSa3F0MzpnIWDFm

grant_type=refresh_token
&refresh_token=8xLOxBtZp8

HTTP/1.1 200 OK
Content-Type: application/json
{
 "access_token": "TxyV34trKY",
 "token_type": "Bearer",
 "refresh_token": "9xLeWTtFg",
 "expires_in": 3600
}

5.1.6.2 Resource Access

Using the access token, the client can access the protected resource. The resource access is similar to the resource access in the first time authorization code flow. For a description on the details, check section 5.1.5.3.

5.2 Implicit Flow

The implicit flow is a simplification of the authorization code flow. No refresh tokens are delivered in this flow.

5.2.1 Usage Scenario

This flow is used for clients that do not have the possibility to securely store the refresh token and ClientID:ClientSecret. This is for example the case for clients that are realized in client-side JavaScript or for some mobile apps.

5.2.2 Features

The implicit flow has both advantageous and limiting features:

- Simple flow, since only one call to the authorization endpoint of the OAuth providers is necessary.
- Very short validity of the access tokens leads to reduced convenience for the resource owner.

- Reduced security, since the identity of the client is not verified.

5.2.3 Preparation

Before this flow can be used, the client has to register with the OAuth server. After successful registration the client receives a ClientID. The ClientID is used when creating new tokens, to confirm the identity of the client. The manner in which registration for the ClientID takes place, is not defined in the standard. In practice, the registration takes place on a website or a portal of the OAuth server.

5.2.4 Sequence Diagrams

The implicit flow contains the following steps:

- Get a token: The client requests a token from the authorization endpoint of the OAuth provider.
- Access the protected resource: The client accesses the resource from the resource provider using the access token.

The token endpoint is not involved in this flow.

5.2.4.1 Authorization Endpoint

The client sends a request for a new access token directly to the authorization endpoint of the OAuth provider using the HTTP GET method. The ClientID is provided as query parameter and identifies the client. However, a ClientSecret is not expected. The parameter response_type is set to "token". The state parameter is simply used for correlating request and response and is not evaluated by the authorization endpoint. Specific scopes can be requested using the scope parameter. The value of the redirect_uri is compared against the value provided during registration of the client.

The access token is returned as part of the URL, which is the value of the location HTTP parameter in a response with status code 302 (Moved Permanently). The URL is constructed by using the redirect URL as base path, adding the token as an anchor using the # hash sign and by attaching the query parameter for the state. The fragment, including the token and all other parameters after the hash sign, is retained by the browser, only the URI without the fragment is used for redirecting.

Note, that the access token is returned directly by the authorization endpoint. The token endpoint is not required in this flow.

50

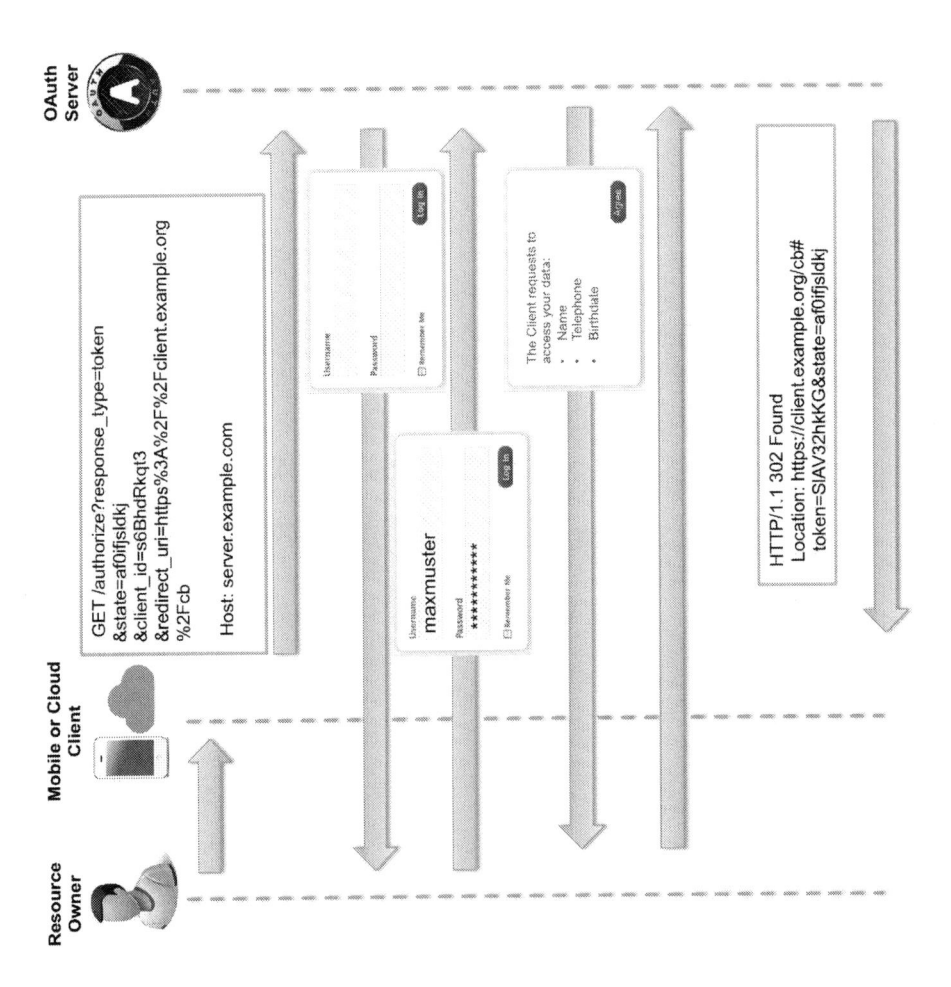

5.2.4.2 Resource Access

Using the access token, the client can access the protected resource. The resource access step in the implicit flow is similar to the resource access in the authorization code flow. For a description on the details, check section 5.1.5.3.

5.3 Resource Owner Password Credentials Flow

The resource owner password credentials flow is a simple flow. The precondition for this flow is that the resource owner is willing to share her credentials with the client, so the client can use the username and password of the resource owner.

5.3.1 Usage Scenario

The resource owner password credentials flow should be used if the resource owner trusts the client and is willing to provide her credentials to the client. This trust is only justified in some cases and the pattern of this flow might remind of the password anti-pattern. Before using this flow it should be checked carefully if the trust between resource owner and client can in fact be justified.

The trust can be justified if client and resource provider are offered by the same organization. The client might be the official mobile app of a popular cloud service; an example could be the official Dropbox mobile app and Dropbox as resource provider.

It is important that the client does not store the username and password of the resource owner. The client should only use the username and password for requesting the OAuth tokens. The client should delete username and password immediately after the request. Only the access token and refresh token should be stored by the client. Secure storage should be used for the access token.

5.3.2 Features

This flow has both advantageous and limiting features:

- Convenient token renewal, since a refresh token is provided.
- Simple: only one call is necessary to obtain access token and refresh token.
- Reduced security: there is no guarantee that the client really deletes the password.
- The resource owner is required to trust the client.

5.3.3 Preparation

Before this flow can be used, the client has to register with the OAuth server. After successful registration the client receives a ClientID and a ClientSecret. ClientID and ClientSecret are used when creating new tokens, to confirm the identity of the client. The manner in which registration for ClientID and ClientSecret takes place is not defined in the standard. In practice, the registration takes place on a website or a portal of the OAuth server.

5.3.4 Sequence Diagrams

This is a simple flow, since the client sends the request for new tokens directly to the token endpoint of the OAuth provider.

The resource owner password credentials flow contains the following steps:

- Get a token: the client requests a token from the token endpoint of the OAuth provider.
- Access the protected resource: the client accesses the resource from the resource provider using the access token.

No authorization endpoint is involved in this flow, since the resource owner provides his credentials directly to the client.

5.3.4.1 Token Endpoint

The client sends the request for new tokens directly to the token endpoint of the OAuth server using HTTP POST. The token endpoint is protected by HTTP basic authorization. The client thus uses a base64-encoded value of ClientID:ClientSecret in the Authorization HTTP header to the token endpoint. The resource owner credentials are sent as form parameters with the parameter names "username" and "password". In addition the parameter grant_type=password is transmitted as a form parameter. The request is sent via the HTTP POST method. The OAuth provider checks the ClientID:ClientSecret of the client and the credentials of the resource owner. The response contains an access token and a refresh token.

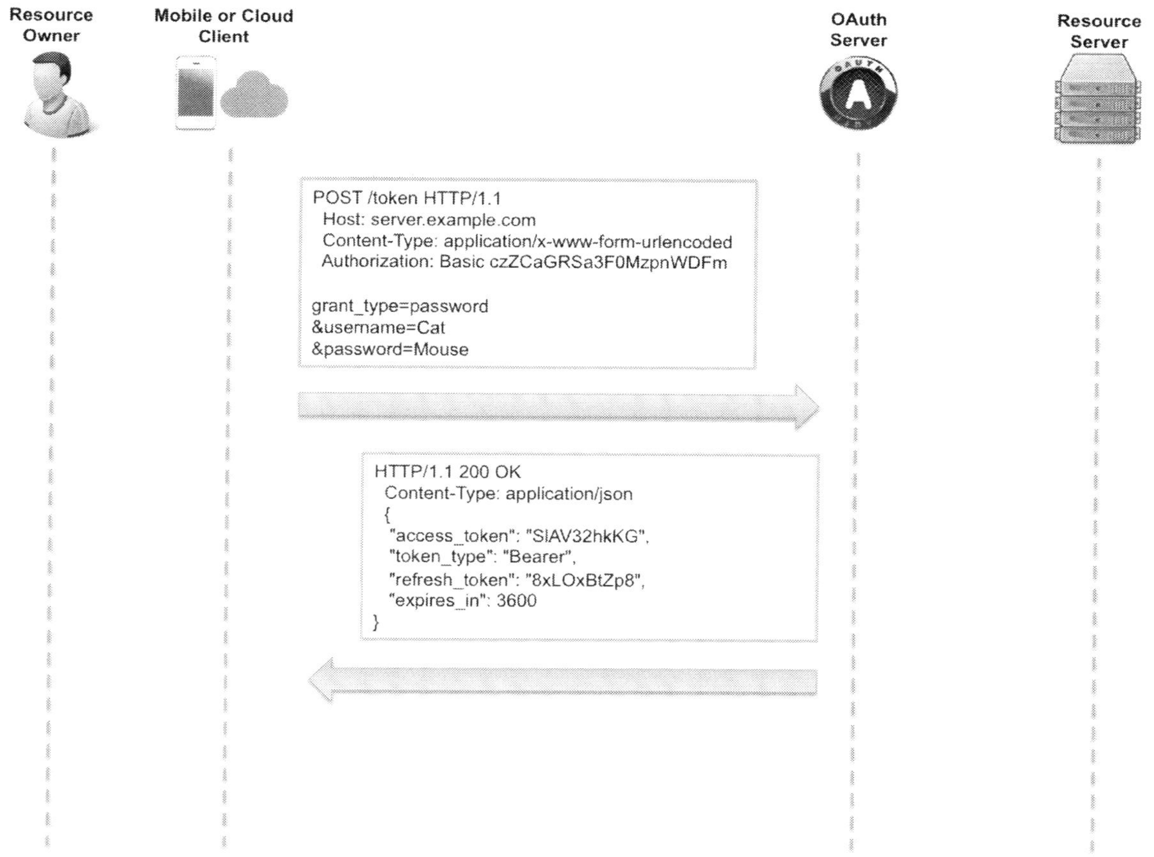

Resource Owner

Mobile or Cloud Client

POST /token HTTP/1.1
Host: server.example.com
Content-Type: application/x-www-form-urlencoded
Authorization: Basic czZCaGRSa3F0MzpnWDFm
grant_type=password
&username=Cat
&password=Mouse

HTTP/1.1 200 OK
Content-Type: application/json
{
"access_token": "SlAV32hkKG",
"token_type": "Bearer",
"refresh_token": "8xLOxBtZp8",
"expires_in": 3600
}

OAuth Server

Resource Server

57

5.3.4.2 Resource Access

Using the access token, the client can access the protected resource. The resource access step in this flow is similar to the resource access in the authorization code flow. For a description on the details, check section 5.1.5.3.

5.4 Client Credentials Flow

This is a simple flow, since the client is identical to the resource owner.

5.4.1 Usage Scenario

In this flow the client is identical to the resource owner. One might also describe this scenario as a scenario without a resource owner. Since no resource owner is present, client credentials are sufficient and the resource owner is not required to authenticate.

The client needs to offer secure storage for ClientID, ClientSecret and access token.

5.4.2 Features

This flow offers the following features:

- Simple: Only one call is necessary to obtain access token.

5.4.3 Preparation

Before this flow can be used, the client has to register with the OAuth server. After successful registration the client receives a ClientID and a ClientSecret. ClientID and ClientSecret are used when creating new tokens, to confirm the identity of the client. The manner in which registration for ClientID and ClientSecret takes place is not defined in the standard. In practice, the registration takes place on a website or a portal of the OAuth server.

5.4.4 Sequence Diagrams

This is a simple flow, since the client sends the request for new tokens directly to the token endpoint of the OAuth provider. The authorization endpoint is not required.

The client credentials flow contains the following steps:

- Get a token: the client requests a token from the token endpoint of the OAuth provider.
- Access the protected resource: the client accesses the resource from the resource provider using the access token.

No authorization endpoint is involved in this flow, since the resource owner is not involved in the flow, and client credentials are sufficient.

5.4.4.1 Token Endpoint

The client sends the request for new tokens directly to the token endpoint of the OAuth server using HTTP POST. The token endpoint is protected by HTTP basic authorization. The client thus uses a base64-encoded value of ClientID:ClientSecret in the Authorization HTTP header to the token endpoint. In addition, the parameter grant_type=client_credentials is transmitted as a form parameter. The request is sent via the HTTP POST method. The OAuth provider checks the ClientID:ClientSecret of the client. In the response an access token is sent in the form of a JSON object.

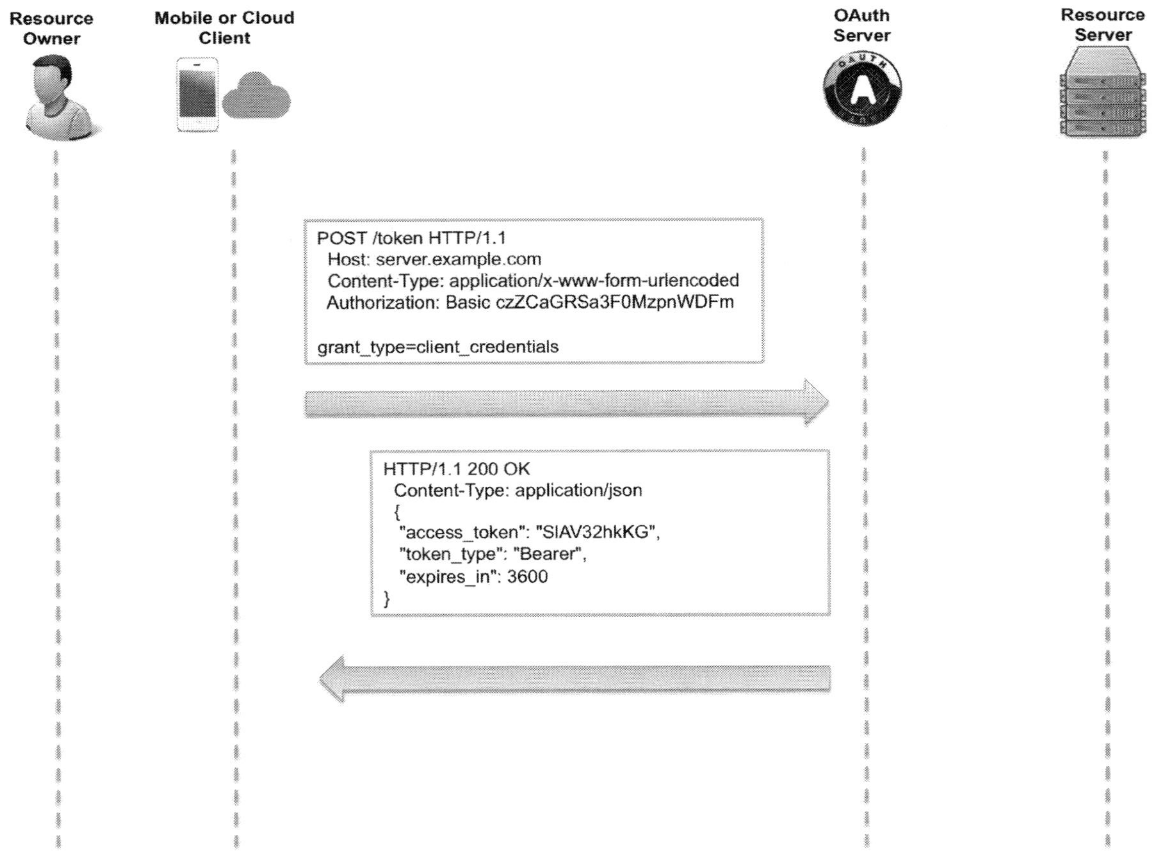

Resource Server

OAuth Server

```
POST /token HTTP/1.1
Host: server.example.com
Content-Type: application/x-www-form-urlencoded
Authorization: Basic czZCaGRSa3F0MzpnWDFm

grant_type=client_credentials
```

```
HTTP/1.1 200 OK
Content-Type: application/json
{
 "access_token": "SlAV32hkKG",
 "token_type": "Bearer",
 "expires_in": 3600
}
```

Mobile or Cloud Client

Resource Owner

5.4.4.2 Resource Access

Using the access token, the client can access the protected resource. The resource access step in this flow is similar to the resource access in the authorization code flow. For a description on the details, check section 5.1.5.3.

6 Extensions of OAuth

The basic functionality of OAuth can be extended by so called OAuth profiles. OAuth profiles are also standardized and they build upon the main OAuth standard. In the following, we study two of the most important extensions of OAuth, the OpenID Connect Profile and the SAML2 Bearer Assertion Profile.

6.1 OpenID Connect Profile

The OAuth standard ensures that there is no unintended leakage of information about the resource owner to the client. The OAuth standard ensures the privacy of the resource owner. For example, it is ensured that the client does not get hold of the resource owner's credentials.

6.1.1 Usage Scenario

The strict privacy policy of OAuth is a good default setting. There are, however, cases in which the client should have the possibility to get access to specific profile information of the resource owner, for example the resource owner's name or address. Of course, the access right to this information is only provided, if the resource owner explicitly consents to the delegation of the respective access rights to the client.

The profile information about the resource owner is made accessible via APIs with a RESTful interface. OpenID Connect standardizes how such interfaces look like and how the data is structured and organized. OpenID Connect extends the authorization code flow, introduces new tokens and standardizes some endpoints. OpenID Connect is a solution that can be applied in many environments, on many devices and with many different products.

6.1.2 Sequence Diagrams

In the usual manner we explain the flows using sequence diagrams. The important steps are:

- Get an authorization code
- Get both an OAuth token and a OpenID Connect token
- Access the userinfo endpoint

6.1.2.1 Authorization Endpoint

OpenID Connect extends the authorization code flow. The only difference here is that the OAuth scopes openid, profile and email are requested. The scopes are separated by blanks and the resulting list is URL-encoded, resulting in the %20 markers seen in the picture below.

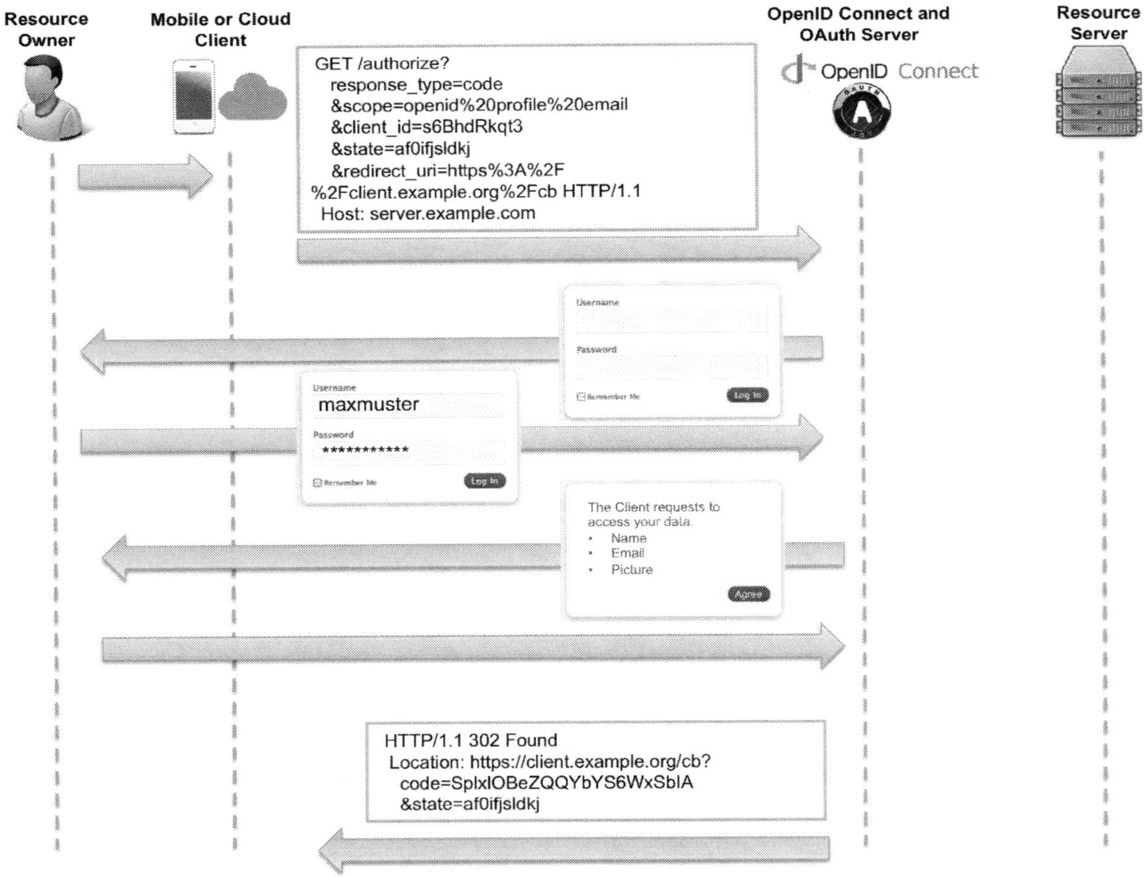
Resource Owner
Mobile or Cloud Client
OpenID Connect and OAuth Server
Resource Server
OpenID Connect
GET /authorize?
response_type=code
&scope=openid%20profile%20email
&client_id=s6BhdRkqt3
&state=af0ifjsldkj
&redirect_uri=https%3A%2F
%2Fclient.example.org%2Fcb HTTP/1.1
Host: server.example.com
Username
Password
Remember Me
Log In
Username
maxmuster
Password
****
Remember Me
Log In
The Client requests to access your data.
Name
Email
Picture
Agree
HTTP/1.1 302 Found
Location: https://client.example.org/cb?
code=SplxlOBeZQQYbYS6WxSbIA
&state=af0ifjsldkj

6.1.2.2 Token Endpoint

The token endpoint for OpenID Connect is based on the basic OAuth token endpoint. The result delivered by this endpoint is an extension of the JSON object containing access token and refresh token. The JSON object additionally contains an id token. The id token is relatively long. In contrast to all other OAuth tokens, this token actually contains information. It is a JSON web token (JWT). JSON web tokens are created by base64-encoding of a JSON object and signing the resulting string using one of the cryptographic algorithms defined in the JWT standard. The signed token is tamper-proof, it cannot be changed without being detected.

Resource Server

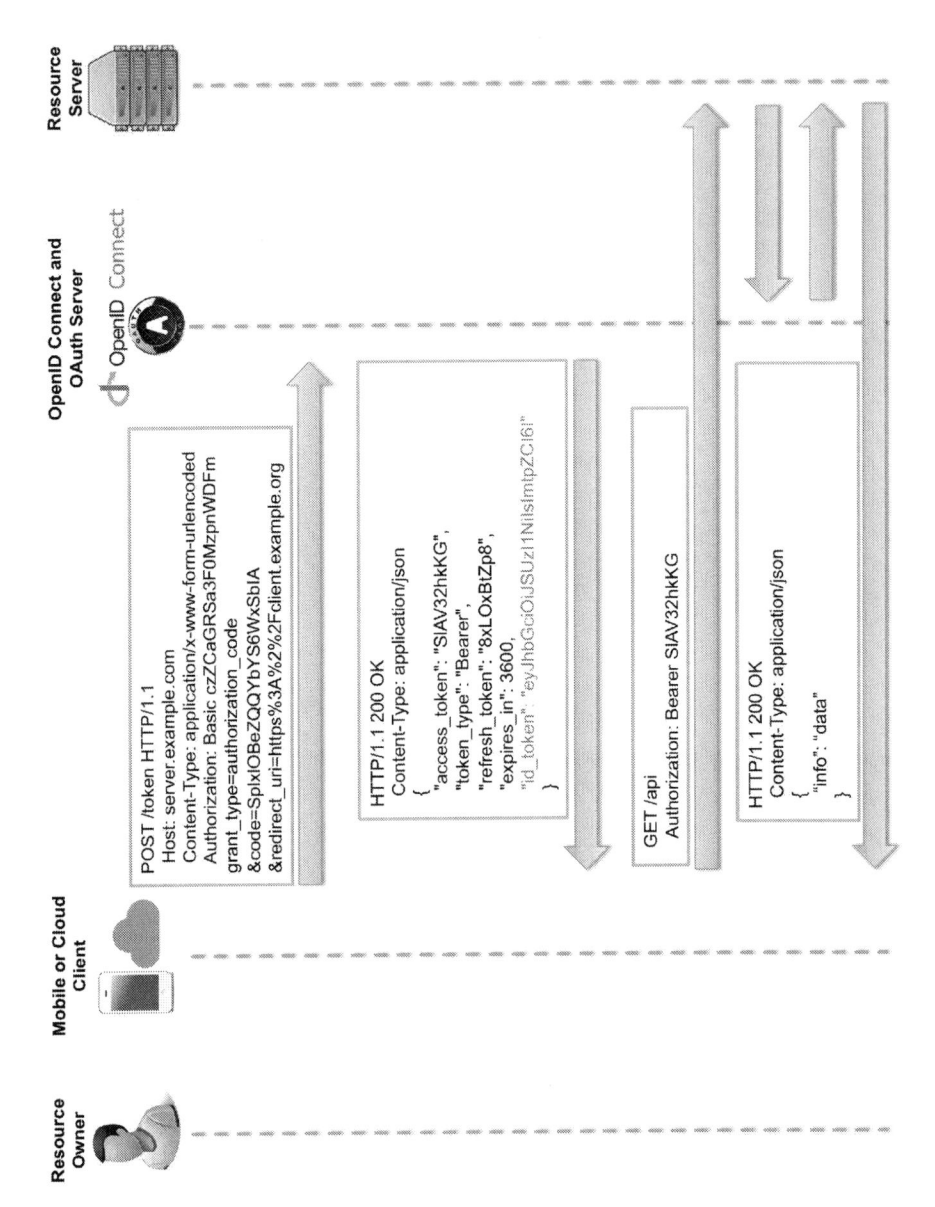

OpenID Connect and OAuth Server
OpenID Connect

Mobile or Cloud Client

Resource Owner

POST /token HTTP/1.1
Host: server.example.com
Content-Type: application/x-www-form-urlencoded
Authorization: Basic czZCaGRSa3F0MzpnWDFm
grant_type=authorization_code
&code=SplxlOBeZQQYbYS6WxSbIA
&redirect_uri=https%3A%2F%2Fclient.example.org

HTTP/1.1 200 OK
Content-Type: application/json
{
"access_token": "SlAV32hkKG",
"token_type": "Bearer",
"refresh_token": "8xLOxBtZp8",
"expires_in": 3600,
"id_token": "eyJhbGciOiJSUzI1NiIsImtpZCI6i"
}

GET /api
Authorization: Bearer SlAV32hkKG

HTTP/1.1 200 OK
Content-Type: application/json
{
"info": "data"
}

6.1.2.3 UserInfo API Access

OpenID Connect offers a standardized API, the userinfo API, which serves profile information (such as the name, address and birth date for example). The access to the so-called *userinfo API* is protected through OAuth. An OAuth token needs to be provided. The scopes registered for this token are used to determine the extent of information, which is retrieved by the userinfo API.

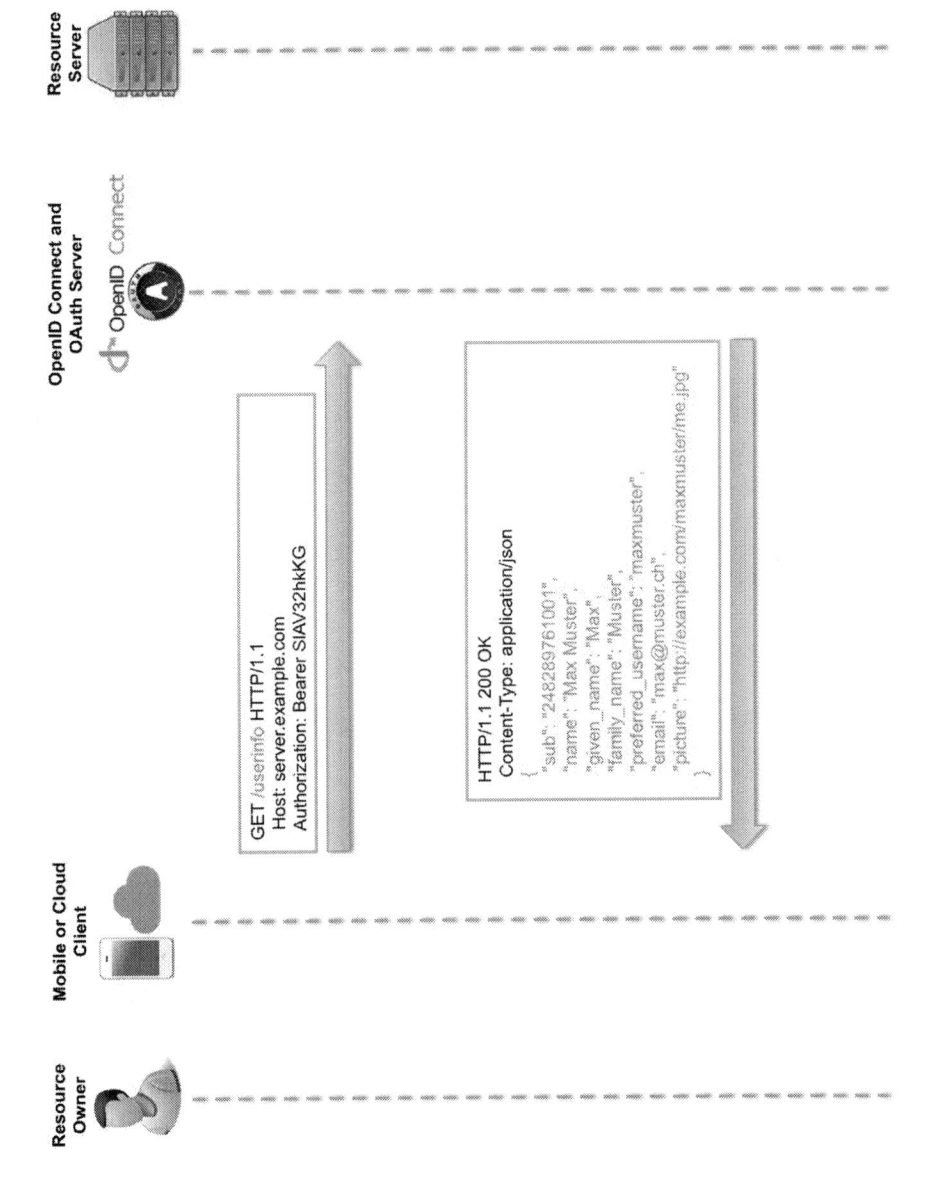

Resource Server	
OpenID Connect and OAuth Server	
Mobile or Cloud Client	
Resource Owner	

GET /userinfo HTTP/1.1
Host: server.example.com
Authorization: Bearer SlAV32hkKG

HTTP/1.1 200 OK
Content-Type: application/json

{
 "sub": "248289761001",
 "name": "Max Muster",
 "given_name": "Max",
 "family_name": "Muster",
 "preferred_username": "maxmuster",
 "email": "max@muster.ch",
 "picture": "http://example.com/maxmuster/me.jpg"
}

70

6.2 SAML 2 Bearer Assertion Profile

This profile allows the use of a SAML 2.0 Bearer Assertion for requesting an OAuth access token.

6.2.1 Usage Scenario

Many organizations use SAML 2 internally for security and web-based single-sign-on. The point of single-sign-on is that the user does not need to login for each service in an organization. Instead the user is authenticated once, receives a SAML token and this token can be used for accessing different services within the organization. The SAML infrastructure is quite sophisticated and allows for federation. Most web-service based products offer SAML support. However, the SAML standard and the basic OAuth standard do not interact well. The existence of services and APIs that are protected by OAuth would not allow for a true single-sign-on idea.

The SAML 2.0 Bearer Assertion Profile builds a bridge between SAML 2 and OAuth, so that a SAML 2 Bearer Assertion can be used for accessing services that are protected by OAuth 2.

6.2.2 Sequence Diagram

In the usual manner we explain the flows using sequence diagrams. The important steps are:

- Get a SAML 2 assertion (outside the scope of this book).
- Get an OAuth token using the SAML 2 bearer assertion.
- Access the protected resource.

6.2.2.1 Token Endpoint

The SAML profile extends the OAuth token endpoint. It adds an additional grant type that can be used for obtaining OAuth tokens. One of the acceptable grant types is the authorization code.

The new grant type supported by the profile is saml2. In the request to the token endpoint, the parameter grant_type is set to "saml2" and the parameter assertion is set to the value of the complete SAML 2.0 Bearer Assertion. This information is validated and OAuth access and refresh tokens are returned in exchange.

Resource Owner

Mobile or Cloud Client

```
POST /token HTTP/1.1
Host: server.example.com
Content-Type: application/x-www-form-urlencoded
Authorization: Basic czZCaGRSa3F0MzpnWDFm
grant_type=urn%3Aietf%3Aparams%3Aoauth
%3Agrant-type%3Asaml2bearer
&assertion=PEFzc2VydGlvbiBJc3N1ZUluc3RhbnQ9
IjIwMTEtMDU...
```

```
HTTP/1.1 200 OK
Content-Type: application/json
{
  "access_token": "SlAV32hkKG",
  "token_type": "Bearer",
  "refresh_token": "8xLOxBtZp8",
  "expires_in": 3600
}
```

OAuth Server

Resource Server

73

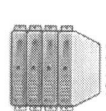

6.2.2.2 Resource Access

Using the access token, the client can access the protected resource. The resource access step in this flow is similar to the resource access in the authorization code flow.

7 Considerations for Secure OAuth 2

7.1 Level of Security Provided by OAuth 2

Absolute security is an abstract idea and cannot be reached in practice. OAuth 2 is no exception. In this section we discuss some considerations to keep in mind for using OAuth 2 securely.

7.1.1 Security of Different OAuth Flows

Different OAuth flows provide different degrees of security.

An access token created by the authorization code flow has been based on information that is better validated than an access token created by the implicit flow.

When verifying an access token, the resource provider should check the flow that was used to obtain the token. Only tokens that were generated using the designed flow should be accepted. The token verification service of the OAuth server should provide information about the flow that was used to create the token.

7.1.2 Client Authentication

To authenticate clients, client credentials are provided upon registration with the OAuth server. These credentials are provided using HTTP basic authorization. In the HTTP header field "Authorization" the values "Basic ClientID:ClientSecret" is provided, where "Basic" is used verbatim and ClientID:ClientSecret are placeholders for the respective values, which are finally base64-encoded.

7.1.3 User Authentication

On the authorization endpoint, the OAuth server provides the resource owner with an authentication dialog. The authentication is typically based on a username and password, but is not limited to it. The OAuth standard does not prescribe any authentication mechanism. Recommended is a two-factor authentication mechanism, using password as the first factor and a text message sent to the mobile as the second factor.

7.1.4 Token-based Authorization

Token-based authorization with OAuth requires that the Authorization field in the HTTP header is set. The value of the header is "Bearer AccessToken", where "Bearer" is used verbatim and AccessToken is a placeholder for the value of the real access token.

7.2 Securing Access Tokens and Client Credentials

7.2.1 Secure Transmission of Tokens and Client Credentials

The security of OAuth rests on the shoulders of SSL/TLS. OAuth should never be used without SSL/TLS. Without SSL/TLS the tokens can be compromised easily.

In addition ClientID, ClientSecret and access tokens should not be transmitted as query parameters, even if the standard would allow this. Web server and proxies might log or cache the URLs containing these credentials.

7.2.2 Secure Storage of Tokens and Client Credentials

When using the authorization code flow, secure storage of tokens and client credentials needs to be provided by the client. Secure storage can be provided, if the client is implemented as a server-side web application. Tokens can be stored for example in a protected database, which is not accessible for any outside attackers.

Secure storage is not necessarily provided by applications written in client-side JavaScript, such as simple HTML5-based mobile apps. Using the authorization code flow for these types of clients is not recommended. The client-side JavaScript source code is available and can be analyzed by attackers. In the simplest case, an attacker can find the client credential directly in the JavaScript source code. Otherwise, attackers can get hints about where to search for client credentials by analyzing the source code.

Tokens -- especially refresh tokens with a long validity period -- need to be stored securely. If secure storage is not available, e.g. on some mobile apps, refresh tokens should not be requested by this client. Only access tokens with a short validity period are acceptable for this type of client. The can be requested by the implicit flow described in chapter 5.2.

7.2.3 Resource Owner Access to Tokens

Access tokens and refresh tokens should not be made accessible to the resource owner, but they should be stored by the client in a secure manner.

7.3 Revocation of Access Tokens

The revocation of access tokens is possible, but currently not standardized. Each OAuth provider implementation may specify proprietary rules for token revocation. One such rule could be to enforce the revocation of all access tokens and refresh tokens after the password of the resource owner has been changed. This way it is ensured that the resource owner authenticates in with the new password.

8 Backmatter

Feedback

If you enjoyed this book and got some value from it, it would be great if you could share with others what you liked about the book on the Amazon review page.

If you feel something is missing in this book or if you are not satisfied with your purchase, please contact me at matt@api-university.com. I read this email personally and I am very interested in your feedback.

About the Author

For 7 years Matthias has consulted large international and national companies on software architecture, software development processes and software integration. At some point he got a PhD. Nowadays, Matthias uses his background in software engineering to help companies bring innovative software solutions to the market.

Matthias enjoys sharing his knowledge and experience in the classroom, at in-person workshops, in online courses or in books. Matthias is an instructor at the API-University (api-university.com), publishes a blog on APIs, is author of several books on APIs and software architecture and regularly speaks at technology conferences.

Other Products by the Author

The API-University Series is a modular series of books on API-related topics. Each book focuses on a particular API topic, so you can select the topics within APIs, which are relevant for you.

API Architecture Book

Looking for the big picture of building APIs? This book is for you!

Building APIs that consumers love should certainly be the goal of any API initiative. However, it is easier said than done. It requires getting the architecture for your APIs right. This book equips you with both foundations and best practices for API architecture. This book presents best practices for putting an infrastructure in place that enables efficient development of APIs.

This book is for you if you want to understand the big picture of API design and development, you want to define an API architecture, establish a platform for APIs or simply want to build APIs your consumers love.

This book is NOT for you, if you are looking for a step-by step guide for building APIs, focusing on every detail of the correct application of REST principles. In this case I recommend the book API Design of the API-University Series.

http://api-university.com/books/api-architecture

API Design Book

Looking for best practices on building RESTful APIs? This book is for you!

This book is packed with best practices on technical aspects of RESTful API Design, including the correct use of resources, URIs, representations, content types, data formats, parameters, HTTP status codes and HTTP methods. It also includes best practices for evolution and versioning, security, performance and availability issues.

API description languages (RAML and Swagger) are introduced as a way to document your API design decisions.

An API development methodology is proposed to provide some guidance towards efficient API development.

http://api-university.com/books/api-design

OAuth 2.0 Online Course

This course offers an introduction to API Security with OAuth 2.0. In 3 hours you will gain an overview of the capabilities of OAuth. You will learn the core concepts of OAuth. You will get to know all 4 OAuth flows that are used in cloud solutions and mobile apps.

http://api-university.com/courses/oauth-2-0-course

References

OAuth Standard RFC6749 of the IETF, http://tools.ietf.org/html/rfc6749

SAML 2.0 Profile for OAuth 2.0 Client Authentication and Authorization, http://tools.ietf.org/html/draft-ietf-oauth-saml2-bearer-21

OpenID Connect Specification, http://openid.net/specs/openid-connect-core-1_0.html

Image Sources

The cover is based on photography by taymtaym.
https://www.flickr.com/photos/taymtaym/14037794691
The original photography is published under the Creative Commons License.

Printed in Great Britain
by Amazon